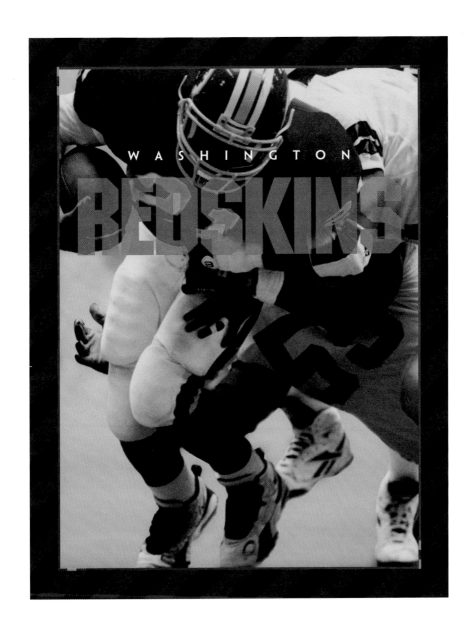

WASHINGTON

REDSKINS

STEVE POTTS

CREATIVE ℂ EDUCATION

Published by Creative Education
123 South Broad Street, Mankato, Minnesota 56001
Creative Education is an imprint of The Creative Company

Designed by Rita Marshall
Cover illustration by Rob Day

Photos by: Allsport Photography, Associated Press, Bettmann Archive,
Fotosport, FPG International, Spectra Action, and SportsChrome.

Library of Congress Cataloging-in-Publication Data

Potts, Steve, 1956-
Washington Redskins / by Steve Potts.
p. cm. — (NFL Today)
Summary: Traces the history of the team from its beginnings through 1996.
ISBN 0-88682-803-1

1. Washington Redskins (Football team)—History—Juvenile literature.
[1. Washington Redskins (Football team) 2. Football—History.]
I. Title. II. Series.

GV956.W3P68   1996   96-15226
796.332'64'09753—dc20

123456

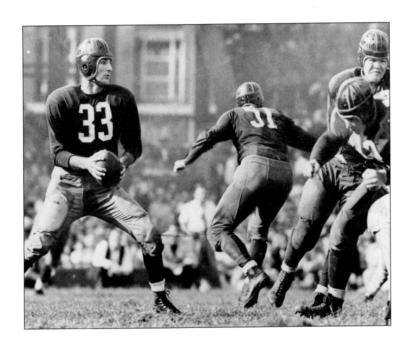

Washington, D.C. is the only major city in the United States not located in one of the fifty states. Washington is in the District of Columbia, which is what D.C. stands for. Washington, named after this country's first president, George Washington, has been our national capitol since 1800. The city is located on the Potomac River between the states of Maryland and Virginia.

Washington is home to such famous buildings as the Capitol, the White House, the Washington Monument, the Lincoln Memorial and the Jefferson Memorial. Washington is also home to a professional football team. In 1937, George Preston Marshall

The Redskins brought championship football to Washington.

moved his Boston Redskins to Washington. The Redskins had entered the National Football League in 1932, but they never became popular in Boston. Attendance was poor even when Boston won the NFL Eastern Division title with a 7-5 record in 1936.

The following year, when the team moved to Washington, Marshall put his Redskins players in glittering gold pants and brilliant burgundy jerseys—uniforms guaranteed to catch the eye. Marshall was out to entertain the fans. He gave them pro football's first big marching band. The band, along with fireworks, circus acts and wild animals, became part of Marshall's halftime entertainment. The team's performance on the field was impressive, too.

1 9 3 7

Sammy Baugh, a charter member of the NFL Hall of Fame.

SLINGIN' SAMMY LOVES TO PASS

Before the Redskins moved to Washington, Marshall signed the great college quarterback Sammy Baugh to a contract for the 1937 season. Baugh had a style very different from most NFL quarterbacks. His powerful, accurate arm was a rarity in the 1930s. Baugh also preferred passing over running plays. During his college days at Texas Christian University, Baugh had shown his remarkable ability early on. "Even from the first, we were amazed at many things in Sam," said sportswriter Amos Melton. "He had great confidence in himself even as a freshman. He was never flustered on the field, whether he was winning or losing."

Marshall wanted Baugh's arrival in Washington to be noticed. When Marshall and Baugh got off the plane at the Washington airport, Baugh wore a typical Texas outfit—cow-

Charles Mann excelled at stopping opponents (page 7).

INVASION! 10,000 feather-wearing fans invaded New York to witness the Redskins capture the Eastern championship.

boy hat and cowboy boots. "Marshall called me," Baugh said, "and asked me to be sure to get a hat and boots. I asked him what size he wore, figuring he wanted them for himself. I never wore a ten-gallon hat or cowboy boots before I went to the Redskins."

When Baugh got to Washington, some sportswriters wondered if the man they called Slingin' Sammy was tough enough for the demanding world of NFL football. "Take my advice," the famous sportswriter Grantland Rice told Marshall. "If you sign him, you'd better insure his right arm for a million dollars, because the tough guys in this league are going to tear it right off of him."

In training camp, Baugh didn't take long to prove to the Redskins coaches that he was not only tough but also had something special. One day, head coach Ray Flaherty was drawing a pass play on the blackboard. He drew an X, then said to Baugh, "When he [the receiver] gets here, Sam, I want you to hit him in the eye with the pass." Baugh replied, "Sure, Coach. Which eye?"

With Baugh and running back Cliff Battles leading them, the Redskins gave their new city a lot to cheer about in 1937. Washington clawed to the top of the Eastern Division, pummeling the favored New York Giants by a 49-14 score in the final regular season game to clinch the title. The Redskins ended their first Washington season by going on to play in the NFL championship game.

A week after beating the Giants, the Redskins traveled to Chicago to face the powerful Bears. Nobody expected the Redskins to win, and their prospects looked dim after Baugh dragged himself to the locker room with Washington behind

14-7. A trainer worked on Baugh, trying to get his knee ready for the second half. Baugh said to him, "Tape me together. I gotta get back into the game."

"They're gunning for you, Sam," the trainer said. "You could get seriously hurt out there." Baugh, with a game to win, responded: "Nobody's gonna knock out Sammy Baugh today. The team needs me. Can't win without passin', and I'm the Redskins' passer."

Baugh returned and dazzled the Bears, passing for 335 yards and three touchdowns by game's end. Receiver Wayne Millner caught two long touchdown passes and the Redskins won their first NFL championship 28-21. A grinning Marshall came up to Baugh in the locker room after the game and said, "Not bad for a beginner." Baugh smiled, though he was exhausted and battered.

Baugh's passing gave the Redskins another Eastern Division title in 1940. Pitted against the Chicago Bears again, the Redskins would see a different end to their championship hopes. George Halas, the Bears coach, revealed a new pattern known as the T-formation, with three backs in a line behind the quarterback. Once the game began, the Redskins could do little to counter the T. Chicago scored the first touchdown and took a 7-0 lead, but Baugh passed the Redskins back down the field. As they neared the end zone, Baugh threw a long bullet pass to receiver Charley Malone. Malone caught it at the goal line, then dropped it. From that point, the Redskins' luck gave out.

The Bears ran up the score, touchdown following touchdown. By game's end, the score was an amazing 73-0, the most one-sided NFL championship game score in history. Marshall was stunned. His Redskins were dazed. "We had the greatest crowd

99 yards—he's gone! Frank Filchock's two-yard pass to Andy Farkas resulted in a ninety-nine yard gain.

in Washington's history, and we played our poorest game," Marshall lamented.

The Redskins quickly rebounded after their incredible loss. They were Eastern Division champs in 1942, 1943 and 1945. Washington defeated the Chicago Bears in the 1942 NFL title game 14-6, but lost 41-21 to the Bears in 1943 and to the Cleveland Rams 15-14 in the 1945 championship game.

Baugh became one of Washington's most well-known people. Supreme Court Chief Justice Fred Vinson discovered one day just how famous Baugh was. A youngster asked Vinson for two autographs. "Why do you want two?" Vinson asked the child. "Are you getting one for a friend?" "No," the youngster answered, "I can swap two of yours for one of Sammy Baugh."

Baugh played his last season in 1947. As the Redskins prepared for Baugh's final game in Washington, teammate Joe Tereshinski climbed on a bench and yelled, "There he goes—the greatest. He's the best football player we'll ever see. Let's make certain he doesn't get any mud on his pants today." Baugh went out in a blaze of passing, firing six touchdown passes to defeat the Chicago Cardinals 45-21. Baugh took the Redskins' glory years with him when he left. Washington fans would have to wait almost 25 years to root for another playoff team. But the Redskins remained scrappy contenders. Owner George Marshall wouldn't let his fans down.

THINGS START LOOKING SONNY FOR THE REDSKINS

Marshall's controversial 1964 trade of quarterback Norm Snead to the Philadelphia Eagles brought Christian Adolph Jurgensen to the Redskins. Short, compact and strong-armed,

Plans are announced to televise Redskins games—the first pro-team on TV.

Sonny, as everyone called him, reminded Redskins fans of Sammy Baugh. Jurgensen had a powerful arm and overwhelming confidence, two things the struggling Redskins were badly in need of.

Jurgensen gave his high school coach credit for developing the strong arm that made his bullet spiral passes famous in the NFL. "Our coach, Leon Brogden, had a drill in which I had to get down on one knee and throw the ball," Jurgensen remembered. "It may not seem like much, but I think it developed the strength in my arm."

Joe Theismann, a quarterback who joined the Redskins in the mid-1970s, marveled at Jurgensen's strong arm. "Boy, could Sonny throw," Theismann said. "If you wanted a tight spiral down the field that would land absolutely perfect, Sonny was your man. A pure passer, he was the best. I once saw him throw a spiral 30 yards behind his back. Try that sometime."

Record rally! Down 21-0, Jurgenson passed for three touchdowns and over 400 yards to defeat the Cowboys.

Despite Jurgensen's power passes and the talents of wide receivers Bobby Mitchell and Charley Taylor, the Redskins win-loss record wasn't impressive. Outside of a 7-7 season in 1966, Washington had losing seasons every year from 1956 to 1968. Knowing that a good coach can make all the difference, Marshall hired Vince Lombardi in 1969. Lombardi, who had led the Green Bay Packers to five NFL championships and two Super Bowl titles, had retired after the 1967 season. Marshall was persuasive, though, and Lombardi agreed to return to lead the Redskins.

"I just can't walk away from a challenge, and this is one of the great challenges of my life," Lombardi said when he accepted the Redskin's coaching job.

As the season opener approached, Lombardi reminded his new team that he had never coached a losing team. "And noth-

Dynamic duo! Joe Theismann handed off to running back John Riggins 260 times during the season.

ing is going to change that," he warned them. And it didn't. The Redskins turned their losing streak around and finished with a 7-5-2 season in 1969. Things were looking up for the 1970 season.

Sonny Jurgensen best captured the team's new confidence. "Just working under this man is the greatest opportunity I've ever had. I told Mr. Lombardi that in five days, I learned more from him than in my 13 years as a pro." But the 1969 season was the only chance Jurgensen and his teammates would have to learn from the master. Before the 1970 season began, Lombardi contracted cancer. Two months later, he was dead. George Marshall died that year, too. New owner Edward Bennett Williams brought in George Allen to coach. Allen had built the Los Angeles Rams into NFL winners. He vowed to do the same with the Redskins.

Allen traded many future draft choices for veteran players. Fans began calling the Redskins the "Over the Hill Gang." Allen made several deals with his former team, the Rams, for linebacker Jack Pardee, defensive lineman Diron Talbert and safety Richie Petitbon. Veteran Redskins linebacker Chris Hanburger and cornerback Pat Fischer made the newcomers welcome. All these players were over 30 years old.

Allen's gamble paid off. The "Over the Hill Gang" made the playoffs in 1971, finishing with a 9-4-1 season, their best since 1945. The 1972 Redskins, led by quarterback Billy Kilmer and running back Larry Brown, soared to the top of the NFC Eastern Division. In the NFC championship game, they faced their longtime rival, the Dallas Cowboys, holders of the last two NFC titles. Dallas had little chance against the fired-up Redskins, losing 26-3. The Redskins' streak was stopped in the Super Bowl by the Miami Dolphins, who completed a remarkable undefeated season by pulling out a 14-7 win over Washington.

Joe Theismann, the club's all-time leading passer.

1 9 8 3

John Riggins holds the NFL season record for 24 rushing touchdowns.

In three of the next four years, the Redskins found themselves in the playoffs, but they could never seem to make the leap back to the Super Bowl. After a 9-5 season in 1977, owner Edward Bennett Williams, frustrated with George Allen's coaching philosophy, fired the veteran coach and replaced him with Jack Pardee, a former Redskins linebacker. Allen's experiment with the "Over The Hill Gang" had meant that young talents like Joe Theismann were sitting on the bench waiting for their chance on the field. Pardee intended to change that. "You can help build the future of Redskins football," Pardee told Theismann. "You've paid your dues. Now it's time to take charge and get this team rolling again. The future is now."

For Theismann, this was the realization of a dream—becoming a starting NFL quarterback. "Some people want to be doctors or lawyers or presidents," Theismann said. "I wanted to be a quarterback. All my life I looked for the secret to making that dream come true."

Unlike Jurgensen and Kilmer, Theismann could rely on both his arm and his legs to beat opposing teams. Theismann was spectacular, but he was also erratic. Pardee found a man who could work with Theismann to correct his mistakes. His name was Joe Walton. He became the Redskins offensive coordinator in 1978, the year Pardee made Theismann the starting quarterback. Walton took the young quarterback under his wing, showing him ways to improve his game. "Walton took the time to make me a better football player," Theismann recalled. "He taught me how to think in a game, how to analyze my technique, how to move."

"Loosen up, Sandy-Baby!" John Riggins taunted. "This is a party."   17

The Redskins achieved immediate success with Theismann and Pardee, running up a 10-6 record in 1979. Running back John Riggins led the ground attack and rookie wide receiver Art Monk gave Theismann a reliable target. The defensive bulwark was massive 300-pound lineman Dave Butz. Pardee won honors as NFL Coach of the Year, but his luck soon took a turn for the worse. In 1980, the Redskins toppled to 6-10 and Pardee blamed himself. "I love the Redskins too much to watch them lose," Pardee said as he resigned as head coach.

Edward Bennett Williams filled the coaching vacancy with former San Diego Chargers head coach Joe Gibbs. In his second year as coach, Gibbs returned Washington to the Super Bowl against the AFC champion Miami Dolphins. Theismann and John Riggins keyed an offense that rolled up 83 points in three NFC playoff victories. This offensive performance was

matched by a peerless defense led by Dexter Manley and Charles Mann. Billed as a rematch of the 1973 Super Bowl, this 1982 contest ended with a different result.

Washington began the game on an upbeat note. Theismann was excited at becoming part of the football history he had watched years before. "As a kid in New Jersey," Theismann reflected, "I wanted someday to be in Joe Namath's shoes or Johnny Unitas's or Bart Starr's. Now, here I stand. Pinch me, I want to see if this is real."

The Super Bowl pressure quickly became real as Miami took a 17-13 lead in the third quarter. Theismann, desperate to spark his team, attempted a floating screen pass over Miami's Kim Bokamper. Bokamper jumped high in the air and deflected the ball. "It popped straight up and I lost sight of it," Theismann said. "Everything went to slow motion like in a car wreck, where your concentration is so intense everything seems to happen slowly. Then I saw the ball. And Bokamper was running under it, like a receiver near our goal line. Suddenly, it seemed like my feet were stuck in cement."

But Theismann didn't panic. Throwing himself forward, he knocked the ball out of Bokamper's hands, making the best defensive play of the game. Theismann saved what could have been a Miami touchdown and the Redskins had escaped from near disaster. In the final quarter, Riggins scored on a 43-yard run on fourth down. Riggins set a Super Bowl record by running for 166 yards on 38 carries. Theismann then threw a touchdown pass to Charlie Brown. The Redskins pulled out with a 27-17 victory, earning revenge for their loss in 1973 to Miami and bringing back the NFL championship to Washington for the first time in 40 years.

1 9 8 5

Joe Theismann set a club record by completing 2,044 passes in his career.

Doug Williams sets up another scoring drive.

Theismann's winning ways followed him into 1983, when Washington compiled a 14-2 regular season record, then won playoff victories against the Los Angeles Rams and the San Francisco 49ers. But the Los Angeles Raiders ended Washington's winning steak 38-9 in the Super Bowl. Theismann lasted two more seasons with Washington before ending his career in a horrible freak accident. In a rough game with the New York Giants, Theismann broke his leg in several places. Jay Schroeder replaced him at quarterback until he, too, was hurt in 1987. Young and untested Mark Rypien was available for quarterback duties, but the Redskins turned to Doug Williams to help them out of their slump.

Jay Schroeder set a team single season record by passing for 4,109 yards.

Williams was a veteran who had shown great talent—and equally great inconsistency—during his long career. He had quarterbacked for Tampa Bay during the late 1970s and early 1980s before playing three years with the United States Football League's Oklahoma Outlaws. When the USFL folded, Williams, like many of his USFL colleagues, attempted to make the return to the National Football League. "There were no starting quarterback jobs available in the NFL," Williams observed. "The Redskins were the only team that called me. What else was I going to do?"

In 1987, Williams worked nothing short of magic for the Redskins. In the playoffs, Washington rolled over Chicago and Minnesota and made it to their fourth Super Bowl. But no one except the Redskins considered Williams a reliable leader in the big game. Williams, the first black quarterback to start in a Super Bowl, realized that some of this skepticism was due to his race. Rather than resenting this, Williams realized that he had a golden opportunity to show his critics that he was a superior quarterback. "My whole life, whatever it was, I was

Left to right: Wilbur Marshall, Charles Mann, Gerald Riggs, Mark Rypien.

'the first of something,'" he told one reporter. "It was destined. It was in the cards."

Williams and the Redskins apparently saw something in the cards that few other observers would have predicted: victory. After the Broncos took a 10-0 lead, Denver—and the whole world—watched in amazement as Washington racked up five touchdowns in the second quarter. By the time the game ended, Washington had trounced Denver 42-10. Doug Williams had a day that put him in the Super Bowl record books, throwing for 340 yards and four touchdown passes—marks that stood until 49ers greats Joe Montana and Steve Young eclipsed them.

Joe Gibbs was named Coach of the Year.

THE OFFENSE RIPS BEHIND MARK RYPIEN

Williams' good luck streak ran out in 1988, when he injured his back and spent much of the season on the bench. The only reserve quarterback, Mark Rypien, was called on to fill the gap. Although the Redskins' defense was torn up with injuries and the team posted a weak 7-9 record in 1988, Rypien played very well. Coach Gibbs had a difficult choice: which quarterback to choose as starter for the following year.

Rypien's short taste of life at the top made him hungry for the starting position. "Whatever decision the coach makes I'll live with," the loyal Rypien said, but he made it clear that he intended to mount a serious challenge to Williams. Rypien won the job as starting quarterback, but began the 1989 season with a puzzling losing streak. When Washington slumped to a 5-6 record late in the season, Rypien broke out of his conservative mold, passing for 406 yards to beat the Bears 38-14. The Redskins never looked back, finishing with five straight wins

Mark Rypien behind the "Hogs" (pages 26-27).

and just missing the playoffs. Rypien ended the season with a Pro Bowl appearance.

1 9 9 6

Ken Harvey is hailed as "the best combination pass rusher-linebacker in the league."

The Redskins began their seventh decade on a high note with a 10-6 regular season record in 1990 and a return to the playoffs. An opening-round win against the Eagles was followed by a 28-10 loss to San Francisco, ending the Redskins' hopes for a Super Bowl shot. But the next season, Washington proved a winner. In Gibbs' eleventh year with the team, they returned to the Super Bowl and demolished Buffalo in a one-sided 37-24 win. Super Bowl MVP Mark Rypien completed 18 passes and threw two touchdowns. Many of his passes ended up in the hands of Gary Clark and Art Monk, who each caught seven passes. Cornerback Brad Edwards added two interceptions, and the Redskins defensive line sacked Buffalo quarterback Jim Kelly five times. A week later, eight Redskins appeared in the Pro Bowl. Joe Gibbs spent one more season directing the Redskins before he announced his retirement in 1993. He left with a 140-65 record and eight playoff and three Super Bowl appearances with Washington.

Finding someone to fill Gibbs' shoes was a tall order. The first choice was Richie Petitbon, who saw the Redskins fall to 4-12 in the 1993 season. Next, the Redskins picked Norv Turner, who had been the Dallas Cowboys offensive coordinator. Turner promptly committed himself to rebuilding the team. Many former standouts had to be cut when caps were put on pro salaries. Although Washington stumbled to a 3-13 season in 1994 and a 6-10 record in 1995, Washington fans and management saw the emergence of some fine young talent.

Mark Rypien starred for the Redskins' offense in 1991.   29

Brad Edwards, ready to make the tackle.

Heath Shuler steers the offense.

Stephen Davis, from Auburn, brings his speed, size and stamina to the pros.

Much of the optimism came after Turner nabbed strong-armed Tennessee quarterback Heath Shuler as his number one pick in the 1994 NFL draft. Turner, happy with his prize, told general manager Charley Casserly that the Redskins were "a better football team this evening than we were this morning."

Shuler came to a team that desperately needed his promise and power. In his rookie season he proved his abilities, setting a Redskins rookie record for passing yardage. He was joined in the backfield by running back Reggie Brooks, a 1993 draft pick who had led the team in rushing his rookie year with over 1,000 yards.

With the rebuilding effort well under way, Redskins fans hope that their team will develop into a strong contender for the 1990s and beyond. The team and their fans would like to bring another national championship home to the nation's capital.